OSTRACA

Johnny Payne

Cyberwit.net
HIG 45 Kaushambi Kunj, Kalindipuram
Allahabad - 211011 (U.P.) India
http://www.cyberwit.net
Tel: +(91) 9415091004
E-mail: info@cyberwit.net

Printed at Vcore LLP.

For Juana, Brad, and in memoriam, Kent

Ostraca are flakes of limestone that were used in ancient Egypt as "notepads" for private letters, laundry lists, records of purchases, and copies of literary works.

The following poems have been published in literary journals:

"Water Spell," "El Cid," and "Nuptial Dance" appeared in *The Chained Muse.*

"Dulcet" and "Figs" were published in *Sparks of Calliope.*

"Sea Storm" and "Thirteen" appeared in *The New Lyre.*

"Danse Macabre" was published in *The Decadent Review.*

Contents

TOTEM

Totem

Don't disbelieve my disbelief
don't grieve my grief.
You, my totem must stand
straight, not straitened
must give fright, not be frightened
ask for offerings, not offer.

I stand where your height
will obstruct the daylight.
I need your face without a face
to tend my subjugation
like embers that flare up
without you moving.

In that stillness, impassive
warm the stones, your bones
and stumps that stand for feet
so they can shelter me.
I know you won't flee
because you can't.

Be colder than a marble saint
shallower than a desert plain
without depth, gravity, weight.
Make no gesture, nor even imply
a conscience that might speak
to me or let me recant.

Be like a plant that never grows
or dies. Flourish without dirt,
air, water, or prayers.
Stay steadfast, as I worship
your blank indifference.
In you I can believe.

Danse Macabre

Abrid las orejas, que ahora oiredes
de su charanbela un triste cantar.

1

Forget the flowers, the pulse, the floozies
the second credit card, the techno club
the valeted Mustang Mach, the free booze

the lobster bisque congealing on a spoon
the wine glass holding a half-drunk cab
the waiter who brought the check too soon

violating protocol, killing your buzz
suggesting you rush to pay the tab
while your mates shift like disturbed bees

about to attack fellow citizens en masse
right as you were toasting the New Year
by raising somebody else's glass

one from which you'd mistakenly sipped.
In the din of ill-advised bonhomie, ear
cocked to the future, you infected your lips.

Nobody knew it yet, not the cute brunette
you took to bed five days later, her lithe
arms entwining her one-night pet

before she found herself a new settee
taking lightly her lissome life
treating trysts as sporting bets

on love, that most elusive quality
knowing that becoming a wife
requires gym-like reps and sets.

You gave the virus to her and several friends.
Now she's dead, you're infected, your life
slipping like a silk tie through your hands.

2

When the rooster crows, you lose your beauty.
It's just that fast. Meanwhile, skeletons
rise from graves to dance, as if the deity

required that a troupe of fleshless, spooky
bone-puppets serve as object lessons
mocking you with orgiastic levity.

Death at parade's head, followed by the duke
and after him, the abbot, canon, sacristan
the common soldier, prostitute, then you.

Your demise, if it happens, was an accident
unforeseen, lamented beforehand
or was it moral proof of a youth misspent?

Yet allegories don't go with our age.
They're absolutes, choices of right or wrong
in themselves reason for outrage

at the universe, which is arbitrary
not even relative, like atoms or pop songs
which admit for every truth its contrary—

don't they? As fever sets up in your bloodstream
and you cancel work and begin to shiver
take Nyquil and fall into troubled dreams

suddenly slave to your heartbeat, pulse, lungs
the beads of dew on your skin, your liver
the burbling in your gut that makes you lunge

for the toilet, you're not outraged at science.
Rather, you find yourself praying to your Maker
seeking atonement, growing a conscience.

3

Contact tracing is a game of telephone.
As you send out texts to your close-held gang
you're requited with silence. No one's home

unless you count a raft of scream emojis
and one leering smiley face with fangs.
It's like when you gave a few women herpes

back when you assumed girls cute, clean and hot
weren't contagious. You gave some victims a ring
but all you got back were threats of a lawsuit

and otherwise, ghosted, rebuked, a pariah.
But this time it was innocent! You even
used protection, but there's none for saliva.

All the same, you feel guilty, contrite, sad.
Your fellow creatures' minds are uneven
and even worse, their hearts have turned hard.

Meanwhile, Uber Eats brings your hot lunch.
You cannot even taste spicy dim sum
a bowl of chicken soup remains untouched.

In desperation, you call your distant mom
the one who never calls you and when she does
it's to complain she's stuck at home alone

since everyone's afraid to put on masks
and play Bunco like they did before.
She doesn't bother to console, or ask

why you're not at work. Instead, she complains
of the mole on her arm, that your dad snores
as your febrile body is racked with pain.

4

In the nightmare, you're freshly disemboweled
unearthed, set in a line. A pan flute pipes
the one the Spanish call charanbela

as one ghoul seizes your hand, you another's
and forward you lurch, with a merry half-step
 a contradance, like those at county fairs

where peasants drank mead, ate roast minted lamb
stroked their loins, picked noses, scratched their heads
looking for lice, and after they joined hands

to wrestle, kiss, wed, give birth, divorce, die.
Their relatives wept openly, bowed heads
Whether in despair, rage or piety.

They knew they were pawns of the deity.
They had no doubt as they lay in bed
of life's cruel, grinding, prankish brevity.

You who has read both Sartre and Descartes
and grew up in suburban sleek enclaves
attending prep school because you're damned smart

and clerking law, how can you be afraid?
The universe was made for you. Be brave
and assume your poxed corpse won't soon be laid

in a morgue, a tag on your toe that doesn't
even mention you hoped for an MBA
a second grad degree to complement

your many victories. The charanbela
sounds again. With hop-steps the black parade
with withered festoons of braided grass, begins.

5

As you awake, the light around is green.
Your throat's parched. You're alive so far
and a single fly bothers the window screen.

Moving like a ninja, you slide from the covers
pajamas soaked, your nose a solid booger.
Gingerly you make it to the shower

where you stand naked in the hottest water
you can stand, naked before the Lord
the Endower, the one with the power

to take it all away, or let you make
amends, be a better friend, not keep score
with promotions, prestige, how much you make

per year. You think about that old word *forsake,*
that corny Bible word, and that other word *forswear*
vocabulary from another age.

Hanging on to the Plexiglas, you brood
how you became a player, an arrogant
social climber, handsome and fit but rude

to those who didn't serve immediate ends.
You never got sick, said only weak pissants
got laid low. It's a new year. That was then.

You're too nervous to strike bargains with God.
No quid pro quo. You have to take a chance
on doing something good because it's good.

But if you get your health back, if you survive
there might be time to make a difference.
At the moment, you have serious doubts you'll live.

6

Your phone is dead, not you. You let it charge
leafing through *Origin of Species, The Rubaiyat*
The Marriage of Heaven and Hell, The Will to Change

and other books you read in college, or did not
or ones you were gifted, their spines still uncracked
gracing your bookshelf, waiting for dust and rot

a bit like you, their covers shiny as if new
but given wind, fire, water or simply time
they'll end up as dust, ash, mold, mildew

without having ever been put to real use.
Opening them, sipping ginger lemon tea
you squint like a sage, beginning to peruse

their contents. bell hooks speaks of feminist manhood
Khayyam says set not thy heart on good or gain
Darwin of man as rivulet of blood.

Blake claims that poison comes from standing water
prisons are built with stones of legal pain.
So much accumulated thought to master

words that you should have pondered on before
when you were strong, unblemished by disease
when your being was less rickety, sound, purer.

It's never too late. Your phone screen lights up white
as if an archangel swooped down from above
to blind you with its awe-inspiring sight.

But no, a friend has said he's sad you're sick
asks if you need provisions, sends his love
and not to beat yourself with a sin stick.

7

You've been absolved, if only by one man
albeit one who didn't catch the crud
but who implicitly speaks for the clan

who days ago, in all good spirits clad
gathered to hark the new year with their buds.
You know you grasp at nothing, but you're glad

that he at least remembers you as sound.
And then, as though a host of fireflies sent
from the merciful open hand of God

the screen lights up with notifications
dinging one by one like holy bells
ringing in a blessed annunciation.

You get a host of texts from all the ones
who'd sent emojis, this time to console
you on the loss of your one-night girlfriend.

You soon begin to weep, remembering her smile
as your friends strive to make your sick soul whole
coaxing you from your cramped crustacean hole.

You vow to be well for her funeral
and if you can't, you'll send a floral wreath
not risking that your infectious arrival

will perpetuate the damned pandemic cycle
and its blind, senseless all-consuming wrath.
For once in your life, be sensible.

The knowledge that you probably won't die
is just enough to make you take an oath
to give your flawed benevolence one more try.

8

A local bar is where you learned to dance
Argentine tango, foxtrot, bolero, waltz
picking the moves up fast, holding a waist

spinning a willing body full of health
less interested in romantic schmaltz
or sex than thrilling at the heft

of one who came to you and spun away
nodding and smiling at your natural moves.
You've never felt such comfort as those days

when you wanted less to take and more to give
feeling you'd live forever, fall in love.
Now you and many others must survive

a different kind of dance, the danse macabre
whether from the pandemic, or because
your perishing is what death craves

as if it were a person with a grudge
a dance master who dances you to bones
like a hostage in a locked, dank garage

torturing your mind and body for pure sport
a dull, diabolical marathon
until you end a prone, spent, face-up corpse.

Okay, you'll dance if you have to, but not die
not yet, until the four-hand song is done
one you'll compose as well, not just stand by.

You put on clothes, stand on the balcony
A blue jay squawks on the iron balustrade
as wind waves the grass like a soft green sea.

9

Weeks later, you've survived and all your friends.
The funeral passed. You couldn't attend
it wasn't safe but sent condolences.

To your surprise, her parents sent a note
Wishing good luck, not assigning you blame
Rather, they hoped for a young man good health

the kind their daughter had enjoyed before "events,"
their word, had stolen their little girl away.
You still grieve her, the one you only spent

one night with, wishing you had the power
to give back life, to wish that night away.
She bongs in your mind like a clock each hour

as you cook for those you love, run errands
ask how they're doing, let each have their say
do small new kindnesses for your parents.

It's not enough, can never be enough
even though no one's asked you to atone.
Your buddies tell you not to be so rough

on yourself. You promise that you won't.
Yet late at night when you are back alone
a soft tune from nowhere comes to haunt

your ears, your brain, soft and medieval
played on a flute, its melody lying
somewhere between sacrosanct and evil

a danse macabre, a permanent background
noise, the faint, sweet gasp of someone dying
who leaves behind a last significant sound.

Leave-taking

You were here smiling and next you were gone
like an eclipse of the midnight sun.

Your stout heart grew too large for your ribcage
like a bird that can't fit its copper cage.

I rained pennies on your hard grave
where they rang like an iron spade.

I sang songs with bawdy end rhymes
To make sure, I sang them two times.

It's late. Crickets protest
that silence suits me best.

It's dark as in your grave
yet somehow, I'm alive.

Soon, I'll drift off
bed cold, but soft.

Pull curtains tight shut
lamp clicked, lights out.

I dream
your name.

You dream
my name.

You.
Me.

El Cid

You're galloping like El Cid, on a flat Mississippi stretch
on a quarter horse-Arabian mix, rented from a nearby ranch
its legs as long as these lines, its withers beginning to twitch
as if a spell were cast on it, by a mischievous white witch.

Where are you going, hellbent, over the cracked dry turf?
To war, like The Cid, who goes to avenge his honor besmirched?
to slay those who pulled his beard, who banished him from his land
and will soon feel the sting of justice from the sword of his raised
right hand?

No, you're riding for pleasure, your back hunched over the saddle
yet you sweat at the crown of your head, as if you plunged into battle.
The horse doesn't know your reasons, only that you gallop in haste
like a hero whose fury has risen and wants to lay the world waste.

Through slash pines and Western mayhaws, the two of you kick up dirt
flecks of it carom off your face and others slide into your shirt
and you wish you had a real enemy, one you could run straight through
but in your black heart, you realize, the real enemy is you.

So you ride and you ride, no end in sight, trying to wear yourself down.
The horse breathes hard, asthmatic, but continues to cover ground
and the rain clouds gathered above you hold off from releasing a storm
as you rush toward a fate unspoken, with the thrill of being reborn.

MASTABA

White-Tailed Deer

I'm hunting a white-tailed deer
rifle in hand, oak stock gleaming.

I waited in the blind for a day
biding my time, but she didn't come.

Now I must stumble through woods
as the moon cruises overhead

stalking me, casting its light
as if to warn my prey to hide.

If I find her, I doubt I'll shoot.
I only want to gaze on her sleek form

and have her glance back, trembling
both of us aware of the danger.

As she leaps away, I'll blast the air
so the pursuit won't have been in vain.

I'll rest my empty gun on a tree
and eat the pear in my rucksack.

Its juice will wet my mouth
while I feel the bark on my back.

As I sit underneath, the gun and me
looking up through the stark branches

I'll watch the moon slide into clouds
like one more hastening animal.

A whippoorwill wakened by the shot
will call out, both scold and solace

understanding why I sought
to follow the fugitive deer.

Mastaba

The rain beats down, the rain beats down with force
enough to cloister me in sullen thoughts
raking the roof, cold, stark, stirring my voice
raising a song that began as a cough.

Friends far away are languishing, sick, broke
dying from causes natural or not
filtering into their psyches like black smoke
hampering how they walk and how they talk.

Their fog malaise has bled straight into mine
vexing my mind, how hands grope strings and frets
ham-fisted, yet bent on finding the tune
best suited to the howling of gray ghosts

the ones who don't scare you outright, instead
wearing you down by hiccups and false starts
until you belch and stagger to your bed
convinced you'll die and leave a fetid streak

not only on the sheets, but in each room you trod
marking each floor with dirt from your dark soles
the ones that spent long hours half-sunk in mud.
You stroke your face. Your cheekbones feel like boils

your nose, a tumor. You know that your brain
has pulled a dirty trick. It's blank neurosis
pretending to be chalk. You watch a stain
on a tablecloth become necrosis

Of flesh. Pathetic fallacies abound.
You've magnified the sound of constant rain
to a vast cavern on a coastal sound
housing the small, hard rock that was your brain.

It waits there for geologists to pick
apart, to carbon date, to scan for worms
for evidence of a mind slowly turned sick.
They'll shield their generation from such harm.

I sip broth from my mug with hard resolve
to not let my imagining run wild.
I'm okay. I'll help my friends to solve
their problems, or make the symptoms mild
although there's not a cure for every wrong.
At least we'll cage the worst dread in a box
black wood, shellacked, pretty, latch and spring
treat it as a toy, a trick, a dumb hoax.

A slave to syntax, I pick up the phone
to call my mom. Paratactic greeting is the best.
Subject and verb, invariant and plain
will reach her most. But sometimes I must test

by urging her to hearken to her dreams
and stir the seeking motion of her mind.
I yearn to spark a dialogue between
us, to show her we're of the selfsame kind

delay the main clause, deflect, stall for time
in hopes that in the pause, she'll snap awake
and show me a facet of a diamond
I haven't seen, surprise my senses

break the brave monologue which has encased
her for years, self-stylings crafted for effect
but often blanched with weary bitterness
that mar the image she wants to project.

A mangy mongrel lurking for a steak
who knows a restaurant won't set out its scraps
choice morsels hasty diners overlooked
until the staff has cleared the tables, mopped

the floor, degreased the stove, counted receipts
and some lone sleepy busboy stays behind
opening a window, letting out the heat
finds the key, deep-sighs, makes up his mind

to have a smoke while setting out the trash
not conscious that a mongrel caught the scent
of fast-congealing steak and waits to gnash
his teeth against a fragrant, still warm bone

one he's been smelling through the windblown screen
no less than poets smell a wilting rose
and sense the fresh, sweet beauty that had been
—like such a cur, I have the keenest nose

for a delayed grammatical main clause.
Awakening my senses, by its discreet
demurral to declare an obvious cause
like rain that insists on becoming sleet

before it turns to snow, with hypo-tact
that sentence gives me hope to state my case
when it feels right, to think before I act
holding intentions in a loose embrace.

Snow lines the mountain's flanks, the downhill streets
rushing with downpour of the recent rain
that has reduced to sprinkles, down from sheets.
Gutters carry runoff to the flood plain.

On shiny asphalt, I walk both my dogs
who ginger-step through shooting six-inch troughs
and calmly hop onto the dry sidewalk
their victory-prance eliciting my laugh.

Children grown, I dwell in a canine world
instinctual, without malice, straightforward
wondering at past madness I endured
and how much of it was stuff I could avoid.

Neighbor dogs spring to fence-links, yap and bark
half in greeting, half to warn us off
their properties. Half territorial
half wanting someone's arms to pick them up.

I keep wishing to be once more a child.
Cynicism muted, I stalk my world
inviting others to put down their swords
wholly, or as much as they can afford.

En route to a New Year's Eve repast
traffic cones and police cars block my path.
Their red-white strobes parody Christmas lights
as they inspect a probably fatal crash.

Wreckage half-visible between cruisers
I feel the ironic sting of life cut short

right at the height of feast-days, bruises
and wounds imagined, wet streets, dry reports.

Each day punctuated, as a bullet
pierces skin, as barbed wire cuts a stray cow
because of its thick skin, indifferent
to the gash, bleed, not even knowing

how the insult was inflicted. I want
to stay alive to the world's constant slights
only not done in, feel everything slant
cockeyed, mean, receive the dagger's swift slits

without being shredded to utter bits.
My dogs' tails wag tandem like metronomes.
We skirt a gutter littered with beer bottles.
We pass a dumpster, shut like pharaoh's tomb.

The Entertainer

He told them he was manic.
They told him not to panic.

His bike went to two hundred.
Around him, headwinds thundered.

He mated with twelve dozen
and hoped they weren't his cousins.

He wrote a book a week
all long, not always deep.

His dog found him peculiar
but hey, he was the ruler.

His ex-wives formed a klatch
to talk behind his back.

He twice tried suicide
but only hurt his pride.

His fame meanwhile kept rising
his ego super-sizing.

His speeches grandiose
made him a popular host.

Until he reached a limit
where all thought him a dimwit.

At last, new medication
brought him to half-salvation.

But without wit outpouring
his friends soon found him boring.

His ex-wives even missed
insane lips they'd once kissed.

But he, at last sedate
beside a faithful mate

told all of them to find
a brand new troubled mind

for gossip and critique
but as for him—he'd peaked.

Windstorm

Far above a cloud mass, caramel-black
and off-white, sleet-clot clusters
in a clime where it seldom rains.
I've climbed high with two yorkies
to watch the desert get swept with needles
of water, forming hash-puddles in brown earth.

I can't explain to pups this cycle of rebirth.
My female dog bites the wind back and barks
somehow making the gusts more feeble
while the male dog growls at the bluster
as if to render the air cranky
enough to flee when faced with sonic pain.

I alone remain silent, scanning the plain
where recent dust storms with ancient-village girth
sweep dirt-ghosts past lanky
ocotillos, driving onward until they smacked
adobe houses, only to shriek faster
as they howled around shuttered people.

Panic to banish dirt-ghosts was needless.
Like an avenging angel soon came the rain
disaster chasing out disaster
while I stood godlike watching harried birth
as if I'd poured sticky liquid from a giant sack
over a campfire made of half-spent planks.

I'm a cosmic misfit, fond of pranks
blotting out the sun with my thumb, heedless
that the land will freeze. I bring back
green fields with a wave of my palm
and in that dual movement, know I can hurt
everyone with even the slightest gesture.

The world has turned. Unless together we muster
the resolve to stop the ice-melt, calm the banks
the hurricanes and snowstorms will grow worse.
Together, as a planet, we're rude gods. Our tactless
abuse will whip fickle updrafts into insane
cyclones, heat waves, and tectonic cracks.

From the steep climb, my legs feel feeble
but I whistle sharp to my yorkies
Who bound toward me, two dark streaks.

Therapy

At my breakfast table, William Blake sits
waiting for a virgin to show him her—soul.
Anything less and the man has fits
since only her kindness can make him whole.

I picked up Allen Ginsberg hitchhiking
after a trucker ran over his bike.
He was hot after the godhead, acid trip spiking
in the threshing machine of his dark starry night.

Sylvia Plath was having a good day
picking daisies to give to Ophelia.
She thrust them toward me to offer her pain
but I only took one and said "Thanks, I feel ya."

By chance, Ted Hughes swung by my office
to smoke hash and ask for marital advice.
I told him I wasn't licensed to dispense
so he flashed me a smile and took out his dice.

Elizabeth Bishop came back from Brazil
with a big anaconda aloft on a pillow.
I made clear I'd tossed her vial of pills
thus her mind drifted to a pet armadillo.

Walt Whitman showed up with hands huge as platters
offering his love like a glistening steak
I asked him if it was hard being a bard.
He assured me he endured just for my sake.

John Berryman huffed up a long winding stair
he and Roethke had staged one more tiff.
A white cascade made the fall of his hair
patchouli his scent, and I breathed a long whiff.

Bob Dylan showed up with a Nobel Prize
fretting that his lyrics would now be despised
I cradled him a while and into his ear
spoke those magic words, "Don't think twice."

None of them reads my poems, but they like to visit
because I'm not like the other artistes.
Down to earth, but they've worn down my spirit.
I bid them farewell to go starch my white sheets.

Haikai

I never slept with dogs
until the thunder
made us both afraid.

Overcooked eggs again
I should lower the flame
but I love the gas hiss.

Driving in the fast lane
until a Maserati
latches to my tail.

Fog slathered on peaks
like cream cheese
and me on a diet.

I'm off caffeine
but it's not off me
an endless chess game.

I lost fifteen pounds
as if abandoning
a tiny lover.

Clipping nails in the sink
while alive.
Who will clip them in death?

Sparklers light up screen
as I New-Year resolve
to use my cell phone less.

Physical therapy
has brought back my shoulder
now to wreck it again.

Biking in Upper Valley
cotton stubble fields
cats watch caged roosters.

Air beats the wind chimes
they dance like frenzied prophets
soon the hail arrives.

THREE ANIMALS

Three Animals

Beneath a bed, three stuffed animals lie.
A tiger, a kitten and a bear.
A floral olive suitcase sits beside.

She was adopted, now she has to try
to stay. The contract gets renewed each year.
Beneath a bed, three stuffed animals lie.

As Christmas nears, the girl remains dry-eyed
in case she has to move to somewhere far.
A floral olive suitcase sits beside.

If she gets past Christ's birth, she'll be okay.
December is the hard month of the year.
Beneath a bed, three stuffed animals lie.

Her mom gave her away from too much love.
The new ones love her too and that's her fear.
A floral olive suitcase sits beside.

She hears them laughing on the porch outside.
The more their mirth, the more they feed her fear.
Beneath a bed, three stuffed animals lie.
A floral olive suitcase sits beside.

Domestic Scene

Down the dawn I climbed, sure-footed
catching the spur of each heel on
the point of a star. I hadn't had
far to traverse, only vast expanses
sprays of half-light separated by
howling voids and hurled rocks.
I beheld you in a bedstead, drunk
with your own sleep, under
stiff blankets like sheetrock
as you simpered and murmured
like a fitful girl in a starched jumper
when she tries to fit into a country
club governed by raucous silence.
But you were only trying to wake up
from a millennial nap, so we could wed
and spawn like guppies in a vast
aquarium, tapping the glass with
their microscopic snouts as if to
make semaphores that might later
stand as lessons in how one era
propagates the next, give or take
a century. That done, we make
a light breakfast of hoe cakes
and tea to mark the bluing of
the sky with tints and dyes
thick enough to drive a stout nail
into and hang the moon on
when night falls and walls

thin into cardboard as we bless
the grate for keeping sparks
inside the fire, where they belong.

Double Wedding

Two husbands within a year's space
her sixteen, then seventeen, with child,
guessing the father by looking at its face.

Stars hang low in a rare, far place
she on her back in a corn-chocked field
two husbands within a year's space.

The first whisked her to a justice of the peace
no warning, no lipstick, just papers filed
guessing the father by looking at its face.

The second found her at her mother's house
abandoned by the first, good name defiled
two husbands within a year's space.

They drove to Tennessee. At least she wore lace.
He glanced at the infant in her skirt's fold
guessing he's the father by looking at its face.

They took quick vows, babe wrapped in fleece.
In his stocking feet, the preacher said grace.
Two husbands within a year's space
guessing the father by looking at its face.

Evensong

I want to write a war song that will scare
all the bastards into going
back home. I want to make it
jagged, without rhymes, the rhythm
jerky, violating expectations, without
stanzas, just pure expectoration
a wad of phlegm but one
best set to music, like a canticle
a candle remade from its own wax
one that feels endless, that will burn on
like battles do when purpose
gets forgotten but you've got a weapon
one that must be brandished or a drone
that just drones on the way a priest does
when he's said the same message over
and over but nobody listens, so the passion
that used to drive his sermons has abated
leaving only words, the ritual, the
outer form to lean on, the way you
lean on balustrades on high, you keep
on yakking about renascence, lest pews
empty, because no matter how slick
the beatitude offered, we all need to go home
to eat corned beef, to drink a beer, pretend
the world is reasonable and all we have to
do is lay me down to sleep and pray
my neighbor won't get ripped by bombs.
I feel much better now, the fit
has passed, it's half-past ten

and I might even sleep, my
breathing's rhythmical, an
angel on my shoulder, fingers
stroking my lank hair, while I rustle
under the blankets
as if I'm the one with wings.

Earthquake, Bay Area, 1989

It happened all at

once. The earth shook
and I threw myself face

down. I was training
for a marathon, endless
minute, my daughter new-

born in our rented house a mile
away. No one else
was at this park, but up
the peninsula a span of

the Bay Bridge dropped into
the ocean, cars too, while friends of
mine were eating beef stew at
the World Series between
the Giants and the A's. I

was supposed to attend, but
through a mix-up I didn't
get the tickets, a blessing as
it turned out. I sprinted home to
see whether my wife and child were
okay. The baby lay in her

crib asleep, unperturbed by the
Big One, until I snatched her
up into my arms, and only

then did she begin to wail, out
of surprise at being squeezed so
hard. Instincts, I guess, and
I'd rather hear her bawl than

wonder. My wife looked at
me like I was cracked, but the
only thing cracked in that wooden
house was a full-length mirror we
hadn't bothered to hang, just
leaned it against the wall. Even
books sat unperturbed on the
shelves, even though we lived at the

epicenter of the quake, but the
tectonic plates had their own
skewed subterranean logic. As with
hell, we don't really know what's going
on underground, we only live with
our fear of the unknown. I wound
up my daughter's mobile and
placed her back in the crib, realizing
I'd broken a sweat running the fastest

mile of my life. I'd overachieved for that
day, all of us being alive and unhurt, plus a
great split for the training diary, if
under unusual circumstances not likely to
be replicated on race day. But no matter, it
was time for an avocado, tomato and
alfalfa sprout sandwich, maybe
some cheddar. I called around and
everybody I talked to was okay, if
disarranged. That was the day.

Karen

If I'd wanted   three hundred tarantulas to cross the road
at once
     while we waited   in a taxi   I would have signed
up
          for the adventure tour   as
it is   I consider this
               encroachment of
the natural world
                         insulting as
     the wind and tides
               eating the sugar sand
the buffet with no hot wings
     the resort fee   the waiter obviously
working a double shift
     with chili stains on his shirt   as if stabbed by an
irate patron

WATER SPELL

Water Spell

A crocodile waits on the far sandbank.
I wade through waves, while my beloved casts
a water spell, a verbal shield to flank
my naked form against the river's blast
in rainy season, mud roiling the waves.
The floodwaters, like land under my feet
Let me cross toward the perilous one who saves
me from the dangers she herself creates
reminding me her love's what makes me strong.
For all I know, it's her, not crocodiles
waiting to eat me, after long straight strides
take me right to her bosom, to her smile.
Thanks to her incantations, I step deep,
eager, as water murmurs, half-asleep.

Figs

Laden with ripe and unripe figs, the tree
I rest beneath, blooming, sap-soaked and strong
its leaves like turquoise, with a glassy gleam
provides shade for whoever comes along.
I haven't stirred yet. I've been lying prone
watching gray cloud-shreds whirl and retreat
as though bruised flesh pelted by random stones
from cosmic reaches by a hand unseen.
My fit has fled. I'm ready to rush home.
She'll cradle my head, kiss the phantom wound
well-made with wasted words twice hard as bone
watch me revive from an afternoon swoon.
I watch for the next new-ripe fig to drop
into my hands, to crush to dark pulp.

Nuptial Dance

Ply her with beer and incense, those twin charms
fragrant at the outset, smelly after
but expeditious in twining her arms
and turning vulgar palaver toward laughter.
You're just a bro, a brute, a knucklehead
with neither bad intentions, nor finesse.
With dull panache you stumble into beds
abetted by each woman's fecklessness.
Later, you're wed to one by random chance
when easily you could have wed another.
You're deep in the post-ceremony dance
holding her mom, while she clings to your father.
Your kids will look like them and her and you
fated to wed and breed without a clue.

Ostraca

I half-expect my poems will end as trash
inside a landfill, far from City Hall
my witty epigrams half-smashed to hash
my laptop left a shattered Venus shell.
No one heeds my deft politics in life
and few hang on my strophes or enjambed
verses, or stop to scan my lines
for metrical inversions or blown rhymes.
But out of those stray fragments, a lone voice
may be inferred, mere melisma perhaps
yet yearning, yawp, a blind inchoate force
a rusted bumper equal to the slap-
stick urge of humans to persist post-crash
as remains remade into silken sash.

Dulcet

My love's voice leaves me stricken with an ache
to hear her half-tones rankle my shook bones
disease from which I won't be vaccinated
not even if her charms seem overblown.
Call me a smitten fool, a bitten clod.
Dig a dirt bier, stuff me in that bung
cover me with peat moss and second-hand sod
but let me listen to my lady's lungs.
If I were a deaf-mute, I might have no chance
but even then, I'd listen for her song
to stir me into sentience, make me prance
as if a glockenspiel began to bong.
Horns of the gods hard-tootle their decree
that my girl's pipes were made to remake me.

Open the Latch

Reeds on my shoulder, I'm headed to Memphis.
Passing her house, I knock, but no answer.
Marc Cohn, or anybody, sing D-flat
as the Wolf River hurries me northwest.
I've only got enough mojo for blank verse
my rhymes and meter are shit on a shoe
flung off the foot of a funky-butt dancer
who tried to kick his ex-wife and missed.
The river is wine, so no wonder I'm drunk.
Memphis is a bowl of bitter mandrakes
and the bait-caught goose cries sharply
while willows and lotus blossoms duke it out.
I'd hoped for a brace of birds to drag behind
yet my traps are empty, so I'll blow town.

The Gazelle

Go to your beloved, swift as the King's steed
coveted among horses, cosseted in feed.
When the whip cracks, he can't be held back.
No warrior subdues his furious attack.
Meanwhile, gazelle flees, desert-leaping
hooves hot, limbs weary, body shaking.
You, hunter, dog at side, strain hearing
to discern its echo. But no, there's nothing.
At river's bend, rubbing your shoulders
sun peeping over clusters of boulders
you surmise this is no way to court a lover.
Subtract the terror, get to know her.
Sitting on a rock for a smoke, you listen
to descry the low wind of her return.

Après

In the long night, under the gelid stars
on Salkantay Peak, in a sleeping bag
I can't feel my toes, as back teeth chatter
my fingertips, pinpricks, my breath a fog.
All day burning calves, from the ascent
as we chewed coca leaves to keep our breath
and sunlight beat until our skin was spent
from symptoms that announce a distant death.
But we revived, drawn by the jagged zigs
of ice fields under which we'd take our rest
drinking cold water, eating half-warm figs
drawn from our backpacks, under bread we'd crushed.
If that's not heaven, there can be no such.
Suffering, redemption, eating lunch.

Arse Poetica

It's the hundred year flood
or draught.
It's dandelion root
    or your granny's pork chops.
Either way, I'm caught
in a gutbucket melee
    running from the privy
    to the privy council
drawers in hand, but no pedigree.

I still carry a change purse
    of Canadian quarters
and field-dressed trotters
    to exchange for political favors.
I whomp-stomp night and day
punching to find ground zero
    so I can start over again
    in a rain-soaked jumper
in acreage where the lettuce greens.

Let's not speak of mandrake leaves
    or inspired rutabagas
unless we really mean
    wham-bang poetics
in which the career objective
is permanently retroactive
    leaving you to yodel
    prattle and prophesy
of leprosies, leopards and jamborees.

Sea Storm

for Brad

If there is a reason for this suffering
to purify, to punish, to reinvent
the mind's many mistakes, its airy
penchant to grandiose fantasies
then let the pain happen, all at once
or in gradual, instructive phases.

Let me parse out the blows in frantic phrases
or quiet ones, meditations inviting
subtle thought. I'll mark my prey and pounce.
I'll curse the sky, retract, rave, spit, vent
until a truth peeks out, one I'll seize
and cup in my hands like a candlelit fairy.

The fatal-feeling hurt at first is scary.
it passes, just as the moon has marked phases
and tides' erratic logic draws the seas
to shore in irrevocable rhythm, sliding
in and away, initial fury hurled and spent
until its heft reduces to an ounce.

A moon-silvered beach remains, where once
crawled growing sluices, come to bury
all traces of land, a flood meant
to bring down cliffsides, but now grazes
like kisses, the stone face abiding
as midnight falls in blue-black peace.

I sit on that cliff-top hugging my knees
face covered in mist-dew, here where I ensconce
my body, mind-spasms gone, pondering
my suddenly vanished soul-killing agony
once a leering death-mask, now, a faceless
stranger on a sand-path who came and went.

My slender conscience makes a sturdy tent
to withstand gale-force winds or a light breeze.
Its fragile yet tough mutability amazes
me, once the victim of blind, bleak chance
now the child of a raging parent grown weary
who sets me in bed, placidly slumbering.

I know it comes again, this force that rent
my life so many times, but its blows barely graze
a being no longer world-weary, only wary.

Così

for Juana

Sun tops the trees with steeply slanting light
as if to shave from leaves their deep green tint
leaving exposed a paler hue of mint
a cataract laid soft over our sight.
Sky darkens, leaving us lost past twilight
as in a cave, matches and flashlight spent
and we cling to each other, in a tent
made by the star-specked velvet night.
Your hand is small and strong, a little thing
of fresh, fine skin, intricate crafted bones
offsetting the immense swell that surrounds
us, the sharp, scribbling sticks and sudden stings
of insects, and fast-falling pinecones
in a forest made from unfamiliar sounds.

Tremors

I
All night the dog howled
lingering and lone like a coyote
watching its own long shadow
cast by the porch light.

II
A rabbit heard the dog
sprinted behind rocks
where it scented
an underground spring
whispering glyphs.

III
Field mice sort acorns
as if reading an abacus.

IV
Empty milk jug skips
down street
pursued by wind.
Soon it will land beside a dumpster
never getting chucked in.

V

Underneath, underneath, underneath.
while not patient
the worm understands
this is how you dig

when your body
is the instrument.

VI
The corpse, soul fled
understands the worm
is just doing its job.
It's nothing personal.

VII
Roofs creak
though there's no air-stir.
could be subterranean
tremors so slight
they can't be measured.

VIII
Cars on distant freeway
constant stream
headlights in dark
slow-motion apocalypse
hum so faint
as not to disturb sleep.

IX
Dog could descry rabbit
as infant senses its twin
destined to be born
seven minutes later
and all it can do is wait.

X
I too attend, wakeful as
the neighbor's dog
when an errant field mouse
scrapes at the baseboard
from inside the wall.

THIRTEEN

Midnight

Begin in utter darkness, find the moon
which has been waiting right behind a cloud
and let it guide you to the crack of noon.

It was there all along. You looked too soon
mistaking it at first for someone's shroud.
Begin in utter darkness, find the moon.

The sphere first shows as sight and next as sound
the thunder's silent, soft, simmering then loud
so let it guide you to the crack of noon.

When clouds come scudding over the inland sound
the water's sheen turns shallow yet profound
then shifts to utter darkness, vanished at noon.

Horizon's curve is bending like a spoon
no path can lead to what's already found
and yet it guides you to the crack of noon.

The hour's spent; a dozen hours remain
to trace the orb's descent beyond the ground.
Begin in utter darkness, find the moon
and let it guide you to the crack of noon.

One a.m.

This is no time for superstitious ways.
Throw up the sash, expose yourself to fog
see what's beyond the clover-smelling haze.

Thirteen fireflies dance in moving arrays
while from the swampy field there croaks a frog.
This is no time for superstitious ways.

In the barn, hung horseshoes gently sway
as if to invite you to cross the bog
and see beyond the clover-smelling haze.

Down the lane in weeds, fairy folk play
or is it the sound of whimpering stray dogs?
This is no time for superstitious ways.

If you rose from your bed, you'd be amazed
at clustering life crowding the lost byways
and seen beyond the clover-smelling haze.

Don't opt for sleep. Perhaps they'll spirit away
these miasmic shades that left your brain agog.
This is no time for superstitious ways.
See beyond the clover-smelling haze.

Two a.m.

You're drinking coffee when you ought to rest
letting its caffeine filter through your veins.
Shed your damp nightclothes. It's time to get dressed.

You find a medal in an ancient chest
that belonged to a cousin killed in Spain.
You're drinking coffee when you ought to rest.

Floorboards creak and shoot straight to your chest
or is it nerves commingled with caffeine?
Shed your damp nightclothes. It's time to get dressed.

Pick up the pendant that your aunt had blessed
the one she always wore to ward off pain.
You're drinking coffee when you ought to rest.

Donning a coat, you walk down the front steps
sliding along a sheen like sheets that shine
you shed damp nightclothes and got yourself dressed.

Now you can ride those sheets into the mist
lettings its spray refresh your troubled mind
you drank coffee instead of seeking rest.

Letting your head fall back, as one fresh-kissed
you open your eyes, perhaps for the first time.
Shed your damp nightclothes. It's time to get dressed.

Three a.m.

Moon waning slow, you walk along a track
following someone's footsteps, maybe yours
treading a path that may not lead you back.

Grasshoppers jump and you're waist-high in stalks
ones you meant to mow down, like fleeting hours
as the slow moon guides you along a track.

What is that you seek or that you stalk
willing to follow for days, months or years
treading a path that may not lead you back?

Dark flashing water rushes down the creek
whispering words, asking you to prepare
as moon falls yet guides you along a track.

How many times will you return to woods
whose paths are steep and labyrinthine stairs
treading a path that may not lead you back?

You pluck a star and put it in a sack
its brightness dulled, as if behind deep clouds.
While moon wanes slow, you walk along a track
treading a path that may not lead you back.

Four a.m.

A rooster crows, two hours ahead of dawn
sending a shiver deep into the sky
light falls upon your shoulders from beyond.

Down in the loam, black insects mix and spawn
scrambling with eggs aloft, thorax askew
a rooster crows, two hours ahead of dawn.

In that same mud, it seems that you were born
covered with slime and crust your skin broke through
light fell upon your shoulders from beyond.

Rough hands washed you in the breath-snatching stream
held you aloft as your withered limbs grew
a rooster crowed, two hours ahead of dawn.

Now your strong head requires a juniper crown
cut from the pine trees forced to let you through
as light falls on your shoulders from beyond.

Algae floats listless on a slumbering pond
with your coiled fist you punch the surface through
as light falls on your shoulders from beyond.

Five a.m.

A truck rattles by. You step in the road.
A man waves out its window. You know that hand.
An early morning ray pierces a cloud.

A duck wanders as if drunk. Here you've trod
many times, in this exact circumstance.
A truck rattles by. You step into the road.

These same cattails waved their green woolen heads
in the same gully on your neighbor's land.
An early morning ray pierces a cloud.

Thirteen ducks follow en route to the pond.
You count each one as if numbering your friends.
A truck rattles by. You step into the road.

The drunk duck turns back honking at her brood.
If you were drunk, you too would join her band.
An early morning ray pierces a cloud.

This pointless point was many times foretold.
You simply must relive it and be glad.
A truck rattles by. You step into the road.

Six a.m.

The bare dawn ground holds ancestors' remains
a humble dooryard scotched by storms and sun
a patch left fallow for their hollow bones.

Those men had brawn, their women had more brains
with or without, they spawned daughters and sons.
This bare dawn ground holds ancestors' remains.

Some were rascals, some preachers, most in-between
cursing and loving, building a farming town
one patch left fallow for their hollow bones.

Many said souls would fly from this domain
leaving their frozen skulls in the hard ground
this bare dawn ground, now holding their remains.

The rest resigned to hellfire, endless pain
wails of the damned, a ceaseless plaintive howl
that patch left only with their hollow bones.

You say a little prayer for the whole clan
in hopes God's mercy might extend to all
this bare ground meanwhile holds their last remains
a patch left fallow for their hollow bones.

Seven a.m.

You're not like your tribe; you weren't born to farm
creation happens more with keyboard flicks
in imagination's endless mind-swarm.

Out of past's poison, you derive a balm
to salve their wound of being portrayed as hicks.
You're not like your tribe; you weren't born to farm.

You live among their ghosts, who help and harm
your quest to rebuild them as if with bricks
or make dense honey from a wild bee swarm.

They shunned outsiders, some minds harsh and hard
a prejudice that made their sweet souls sick.
You're not like your tribe; you weren't born to farm.

Yet you wish you had tilled the land like them
hoe beside hoe, you'd find the common ground
in imagination's endless mind-swarm.

You know their flaws yet want to share their lives
to stir that sauce to render it sweet, thick.
You're not like your tribe; you weren't born to farm
except in imagination's endless mind-swarm.

Eight a.m.

Late breakfast; you make sizzling eggs and grits
holding your spatula like a small hoe
flipping your ham like dark, rich dirt.

In the iron skillet, grease pops and spits
as you give the handle stronger elbow.
Late breakfast; you hear sizzling eggs and grits.

Pages remain by day's end to get writ
your rooster like a second conscience crows
as you flip your ham like dark, rich dirt.

Your kin say art's less work than sugar-tit
taking less sheer grit than tobacco to grow
late breakfast; you hear sizzling eggs and grits.

If you'd just write a movie, they'd see it
but a book of poems ain't exactly a show
so you flip your ham like dark, rich dirt.

Once they find out their lives are in the script
of poems, they'll crack the plank-stiff spine for sure.
Meanwhile just eat your sizzling eggs and grits
stabbing at your thick ham like dark, rich dirt.

Nine a.m.

The dream within the dream within the dream
is where you aim when you sit down to write
cocoon within cocoon within cocoon.

In that dense incense cloud there is no night
or day, no midday sun nor any midnight
just dream within the dream within the dream.

Others set out to work in banks or clean
houses, but your game, spiked spirit takes flight
into cocoon, cocoon within cocoon.

For others, sphere esoteric, for you plain
sense, where you were, will be, have always been
the dream within the dream within the dream.

Knowledge you don't know how to explain
rather, you live it, endure it, abide
cocoon within cocoon within cocoon

Three is three, six six and nine is nine
unknown is known, heard unheard, unseen seen,
the dream's within the dream within the dream
cocoon within cocoon within cocoon.

Ten a.m.

Do the dishes, take out trash, wash shirts.
Hours have passed, you parked at your desk
only minutes since you began to work.

Nobody rang the doorbell, none there lurks
to sell solar panels, a satellite dish
do your dishes, take out trash, wash shirts.

You're hungry; even your stomach gurgles
as if it were afternoon. That's a wish.
It's only minutes since you began to work.

You don't possess a body; mind comes first.
Come to the end of the poem, after which
do the dishes, take out trash, wash shirts.

Your mind's a cycle, just like the washer
its movement is a churn, a pulse, a swish
only minutes since you began to work.

Vaguely you're aware your shoulders hurt.
Discomfort is just a word, a concept, next
do the dishes, take out trash, wash shirts
only minutes since you began to work.

11 a.m.

'Tis the year's midnight, and it is the day's
that's what John Donne said on Saint Lucy's feast
the sun sends forth light squibs, no constant rays.

And even though it's eleven, by your clock's face
the weather's just as he described, light weak
'tis the year's midnight, and it is the day's.

You feel as though you're finished for always
though by the world's schedule you haven't peaked
and sun sends forth light squibs, no constant rays.

You wish for definition, as midday
when lunch means lunch, when west doesn't mean east
yet it's the year's midnight, also the day's.

Eleven is when people start to praise
their Maker, twelve is when they often cease
while sun sends forth light squibs, no constant rays.

Hasten to church; meet neighbors on the way
put all your skeptical humor in a purse
though the year's midnight, and it is the day's
and sun sends forth light squibs, no constant rays.

Noon

You sit in the wayside church's last pew
taking in crucifixion on stained glass.
It strangely cheers you, like fresh morning dew.

The pastor speaks, not directly to you
on this day, he'll give heretics a pass
as you sit in the wayside church's final pew.

All he wants to do is share the good news
resurrection, salvation and all that.
It strangely cheers you, like fresh morning dew.

In your own way you're mystics, he and you
divining blind what you can't outright guess
where you sit in the wayside church's final pew.

You gave in to the mystery long ago
giving to spirit what the brain bypasses.
It strangely cheers you, like fresh morning dew.

No time for gloom, you let submerged joy show
grasping at neighbors' hands when peace is passed.
You sit in the wayside church's last pew.
It strangely cheers you, like fresh morning dew.